Date: 2/1/18

World Book's Learning Ladders

World of Birds

WORLD BOOK

www.worldbook.com

World Book, Inc.
180 North LaSalle Street
Suite 900
Chicago, Illinois 60601
USA

For information about other World Book publications, visit our website at **www.worldbook.com** or call **1-800-WORLDBK (967-5325)**.

For information about sales to schools and libraries, call **1-800-975-3250 (United States)**; **1-800-837-5365 (Canada)**.

Library of Congress Cataloging-in-Publication Data for this volume has been applied for.

World Book's Learning Ladders
ISBN 978-0-7166-7945-5 (set, hc.)

World of Birds
ISBN 978-0-7166-7955-4 (hc.)

Also available as:
ISBN 978-0-7166-7965-3 (e-book)

Printed in China by Shenzhen Wing King Tong Paper Products Co, Ltd., Shenzhen, Guangdong
1st printing December 2017

Staff

Executive Committee
President: Jim O'Rourke
Vice President and Editor in Chief: Paul A. Kobasa
Vice President, Finance: Donald D. Keller
Vice President, Marketing: Jean Lin
Vice President, International Sales: Maksim Rutenberg
Vice President, Technology: Jason Dole
Director, Human Resources: Bev Ecker

Editorial
Director, New Print Publishing: Tom Evans
Senior Editor, New Print Publishing: Shawn Brennan
Writer: Jacqueline Jasek
Director, Digital Product Content Development: Emily Kline
Manager, Indexing Services: David Pofelski
Manager, Contracts & Compliance (Rights & Permissions): Loranne K. Shields
Librarian: S. Thomas Richardson

Digital
Director, Digital Product Development: Erika Meller
Digital Product Manager: Jonathan Wills

Graphics and Design
Senior Art Director: Tom Evans
Coordinator, Design Development and Production: Brenda Tropinski
Senior Visual Communications Designer: Melanie J. Bender
Media Researcher: Rosalia Bledsoe

Manufacturing/Pre-Press
Manufacturing Manager: Anne Fritzinger
Proofreader: Nathalie Strassheim

Photographic credits: Cover: © Mrinal Pal, Shutterstock; © Dreamstime: 12, 18; © Shutterstock: 4, 7, 8, 11, 14, 16, 20, 22, 26, 27.

Illustrators: WORLD BOOK illustrations by Quadrum Ltd

What's inside?

This book tells you about some beautiful and interesting birds that live around the world. Some live in your own backyard—and some may even live in your home as pets!

Songbirds

Spring has come! Listen to the birds sing! Noisy songbirds have been busy making their nests. *Peep! Peep!* Baby birds are being born!

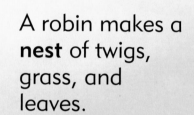

A robin makes a **nest** of twigs, grass, and leaves.

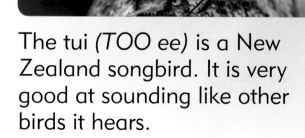

The tui *(TOO ee)* is a New Zealand songbird. It is very good at sounding like other birds it hears.

he father feeds
he **chicks** while
he mother gets
more food.

he robin's
lue **eggs**
ill soon
atch.

The male robin
has a bright
red **breast**.

It's a fact!

In most songbirds,
only the males
can sing.

Water birds

Swans are graceful swimmers. Like many other water birds, they can also walk and fly. But watch out if you make this one mad! It will hiss loudly!

A swan has a short **tail**. · · · · · · · · · · · ·

A long **neck** · · · · · · · · · · · helps a swan reach plants underwater to eat.

It's a fact!
Most ducklings (baby ducks) can swim and run on the day they hatch, but they cannot fly for several weeks.

Geese are fast fliers as well as strong swimmers. They fly to warmer places when the weather gets cold. Geese form a v as they fly together in the sky.

Water rolls off the swan's **feathers.**

Webbed feet make the swan a good swimmer.

Wading birds

Look at all the pink flamingos *(fluh MIHNG gohz)*! These birds with long legs live in large groups. Like other wading birds, they live near lakes, marshes, and seas. Flamingoes live all over the world.

The spoonbill is a wading bird that swings its spoon-shaped bill from side to side in the water in search of food.

A flamingo stands on one leg and curves its long **neck** to preen (fluff) its feathers with its bill.

The legend that a stork brings the new baby into the home comes from the fact that this wading bird takes loving care of its own young.

The flamingo gets its bright pink **feathers** from eating shellfish.

A flamingo wades through the water with its long **legs**.

curved **bill** helps a flamingo pull food from the sand.

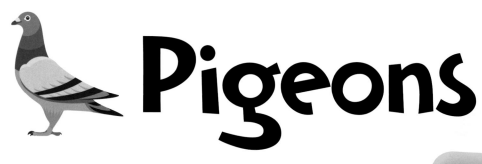

Pigeons

Pigeons *(PIHJ uhnz)* live wild all around the world. Some people once trained pigeons to carry messages written on bits of paper. Some people race their pet pigeons. Pigeons are fast, powerful fliers.

It's a fact!

People have long regarded the dove as a symbol of peace.

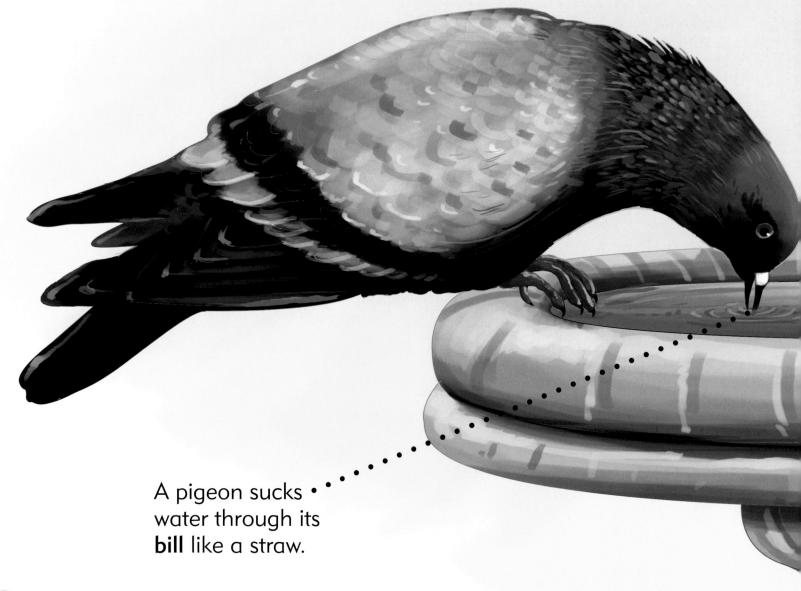

A pigeon sucks water through its **bill** like a straw.

A **dove** is a type of small pigeon. The mourning dove was named for the sad cooing sound made by the male.

Powerful **wings** make the pigeon a fast flier.

A pigeon has short, strong **legs**.

Woodpeckers

Knock-knock! Who's there? A woodpecker—up in the tree! This bird pecks on the tree bark to make a hole. It looks and listens for a tasty insect to eat.

A woodpecker drills a hole in the tree bark with its sharp **beak.**. It uses its long, sticky tongue to pull out an insect.

Strong **feet** and sharp **claws** help the bird cling to the tree bark.

The yellow-bellied sapsucker is a type of woodpecker. Like many other woodpeckers, it eats berries and nuts, as well as insects. This bird got its name because it also drills holes to sip sap from trees. Sap is a liquid that flows in trees.

It's a fact!

Most male woodpeckers have some red feathers on their head.

The bird uses its stiff **tail feathers** to help hold its body against the tree.

13

Farm birds

Gobble-gobble! Turkeys are large North American birds. Farmers raise them for their meat. A male turkey is called a tom. *Cock-a-doodle-doo!* A male chicken is called a rooster. Female turkeys and chickens are called hens. Chickens are raised on farms all over the world for their meat and eggs.

A long, loose piece of skin called a **wattle** •• hangs around the neck.

Chicken eggs hatch after 21 to 22 days. Baby chicks are covered with short, fluffy feathers called down.

A beardlike tuft of **feathers** hangs from the tom's breas

A tom turkey has a reddish **head** and **neck**.

Farm turkeys cannot fly. They get too heavy for their **wings** to support them.

The rooster has a red **comb** on top of its head.

It's a fact!

The Jersey Giant is the biggest chicken. A grown-up rooster weighs up to 13 pounds (5.9 kilograms)!

Birds that hunt

An eagle swoops down to catch a fish right out of the water! Hunting birds are called birds of prey or raptors. There are hundreds of kinds of birds of prey, and they eat many kinds of animals. Birds of prey also include falcons, hawks, owls, and vultures.

Powerful, wide **wings** make the eagle a strong, graceful flyer.

Most owls hunt for food at night. But snowy owls hunt during the day. This is because nights are short in the Arctic where they live.

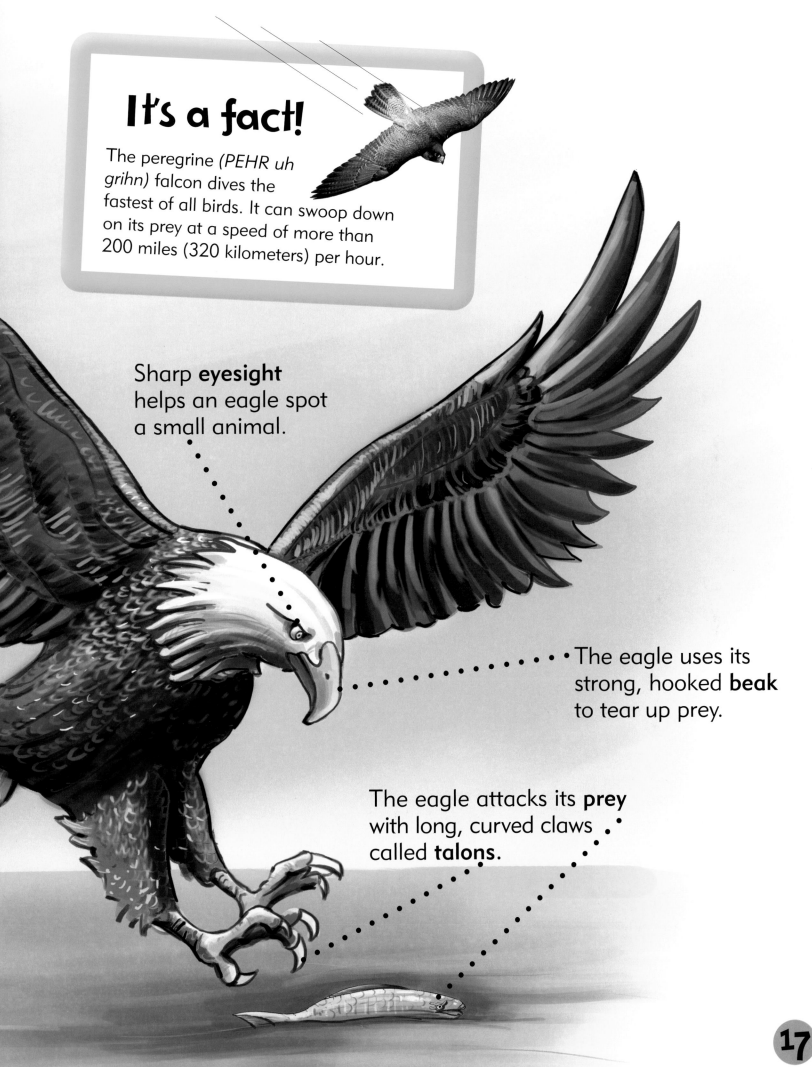

It's a fact!

The peregrine *(PEHR uh grihn)* falcon dives the fastest of all birds. It can swoop down on its prey at a speed of more than 200 miles (320 kilometers) per hour.

Sharp **eyesight** helps an eagle spot a small animal.

The eagle uses its strong, hooked **beak** to tear up prey.

The eagle attacks its **prey** with long, curved claws called **talons**.

Parrots

Parrots live where it is warm all the time. Most parrots have brightly colored feathers. They are noisy and intelligent birds. They are also popular pets. Many parrots can be taught to talk. These parrots are macaws *(muh KAWZ)*. Macaws are the largest parrots in the world.

A heavy, powerful **beak** helps the bird crack open and eat nuts, seeds, and fruit.

Colorful **feathers** help the macaw blend in with the leaves, flowers, and fruits of the rain forest.

The kakapo *(KAH kuh poh)* is a large, rare parrot that lives in New Zealand. It is different from other parrots because it cannot fly.

Strong **feet** help the macaw to grab fruit and nuts and climb trees.

It's a fact!

The gray parrot can learn new phrases with only a few hours of teaching.

Birds that don't fl

All birds have feathers. But not all birds can fly. Some birds, such as ostriches *(AWS trihch uhz)*, emus *(EE myooz)*, and rheas *(REE uhz)*, can only walk or run. They use their wings for balance when they are walking or running. Penguins *(PEHN gwihnz)* use their wings to "fly" underwater rather than in the air!

The kiwi *(KEE wee)* lives in New Zealand. It has only a few stiff feathers for wings, so it cannot fly. The kiwi's long beak helps it feed on earthworms, insects, and berries.

The bird has a long, bullet-shaped **body**.

Short, thick **feathers** cover the penguin's body.

A penguin waddles on its short **legs**.

A penguin uses its **wings** as flippers in the water.

It's a fact!

The male African ostrich is the largest bird. It may grow as tall as 8 feet (2.4 meters) and weigh as much as 345 pounds (156 kilograms). But it cannot fly.

Pet birds

People have long kept birds as pets. A canary *(kuh NAIR ee)* is a popular bird pet. People keep canaries for their beautiful singing, and because they make cheerful companions. Most pet canaries are bright yellow.

The cage should be big enough for the bird to fly and exercise.

A canary eats mainly **seeds..** ·······

A bird's **cage** ·······
must be kept clean.

The budgerigar *(buhj uhr ee GAHR)*, or budgie, is a type of small parakeet. The budgie is a popular bird pet because it can be trained to talk and whistle. It comes in many colors.

It's a fact!

Pet cockatoos *(KOK uh tooz)* may live for 50 years.

A pet bird should always have fresh **water** for drinking.

Lots of **toys** keep a pet bird happy.

You should also feed your canary leafy **greens,** other vegetables, and fruit.

At the pond

A pond is a place where you can see many kinds of birds. What kinds of birds do you see?

Words you know

Here are some words that you learned earlier. Say them out loud, then try to find the things in the picture.

feathers   wing

nest   beak

egg   chick

24

How many eggs are in the nest?

How many pigeons do you see?

Did you know?

The emperor penguin is the deepest diver of all birds. It can dive to nearly 2,000 feet (610 meters) underwater.

Arctic terns migrate farther than any other bird. They travel about 11,000 miles (17,700 kilometers) each way between their breeding grounds in the Arctic and winter home in the Antarctic.

The showy peacock is related to chickens, turkeys, and pheasants.

The highest flyer is the bar-headed goose. Some flocks of bar-headed geese fly over the world's highest mountain range, the Himalaya in Asia, at a height of more than 25,000 feet (7,625 meters).

Baby pigeons and doves are called squeakers.

Most scientists think that birds developed from small, meat-eating dinosaurs.

Puzzles

Close-up!

We've zoomed in on parts of three birds' bodies. Can you figure out which bird you are looking at?

1

2

3

Double trouble!

These two pictures are not exactly the same. What are five things in picture b that are different from picture a?

a

b

Answers on page 32.

Match up!

Match each word on the left with its picture on the right.

1. penguin

2. swan

3. pigeon

4. robin

5. eagle

6. canary

a

b

c

d

e

f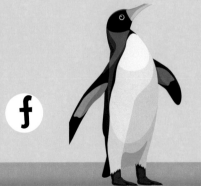

Answers on page 32.

True or false

Which of these sentences is true? Turn to the page numbers shown for help.

1 A male turkey is called a tom. **Go to page 14.**

2 The flamingo gets its bright pink feathers from chewing bubblegum. **Go to page 9.**

3 Swans cannot fly. **Go to page 6.**

4 Penguins cannot fly. **Go to page 20.**

5 All birds have feathers. **Go to page 20.**

Answers on page 32.

Find out more

Books

ABC Birds by the American Museum of Natural History (Sterling Publishing, 2016)
From Albatross to Zebra Finch, this oversize ABC board book, developed in conjunction with the American Museum of Natural History, celebrates 26 beautiful birds.

Bird Guide of North America by Jonathan Alderfer (National Geographic Society, 2013)
Featuring 100 species of birds from coast to coast, this colorful guide helps kids identify and understand birds.

National Geographic Little Kids First Big Book of Birds by Catherine D. Hughes (National Geographic Society, 2016)
This book introduces young readers to birds of all kinds. More than 100 colorful photos are paired with profiles of each bird, along with facts about the creatures' sizes, diets, homes, and more.

Ultimate Explorer Field Guide: Birds by Julie Beer (National Geographic Society, 2016)
This fun, photo-filled, and fact-packed bird guide will help kids find feathered friends right in their own backyards.

Websites

All About Birds
http://www.enchantedlearning.com/subjects/birds/
Enchanted Learning gives both basic and extraordinary facts about birds, bird symbols and pictures, bird jokes, and crafts.

The Backyard Birder
http://bird-birding.ca/
Begin watching birds in your backyard with a bird feeder, following the guidance of this website.

Cornell Lab of Ornithology – BirdSleuth
http://www.birdsleuth.org/
This website from the Cornell Lab of Ornithology is a great introduction to birding for K-12 students and teachers as well as parents. It features educational resources, workshops and webinars, a guide to the best birding apps for kids, and more.

National Geographic Kids
http://kids.nationalgeographic.com/animals/hubs/birds/
Learn about all kinds of birds on this website featuring photos, videos, and games.

Answers

Puzzles
from pages 28 and 29

Close-up!
1. turkey
2. penguin
3. eagle

Double trouble!
In picture b, the parrot's tail feathers are longer, the green feathers on the parrot's wing changed to yellow, a flying falcon was added to the background, orange leaves were added in the bottom right corner, and the blue flowers on the lower left are larger.

Match up!
1. f   4. e
2. d   5. a
3. c   6. b

True or false
from page 30

1. true
2. false
3. false
4. true
5. true

Index